JOBS AT ALL HOURS

BY SUSAN BLACKABY

Harcourt

Orlando   Boston   Dallas   Chicago   San Diego

Visit *The Learning Site!*

www.harcourtschool.com

There are all kinds of jobs
you can have. There are jobs that
last all day. There are jobs that
last all night.

Some jobs start in the afternoon. Some jobs start at night. Some jobs continue all hours.

I am ready to start my job
in the afternoon. Late at night,
I am still working. I keep the
school in good shape for you.

4

We fix the streets. We start
working when there are few
cars on the road, after rush hour.
Then we fill holes and spread tar
on the road.

I bake bread in the middle of
the night. My bread is ready for
breakfast. When you go to school,
I go to bed instead!

6

I am a farmer. I am up hours before the sun! I work in the meadow while you are in bed.

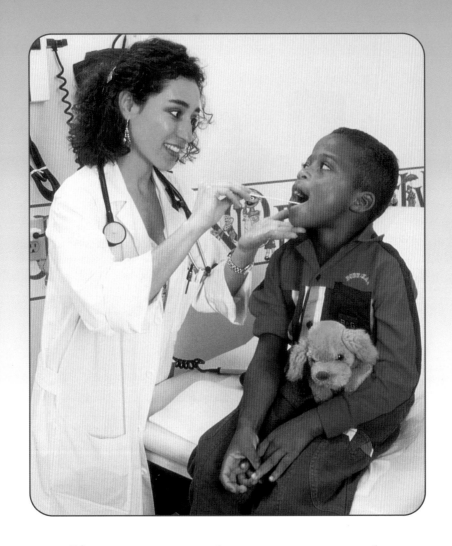

If you are sick, we are ready to help. We are on the job at all hours. If you need care, we are here.

I drive a big, heavy truck. It can carry a lot of bread. If I get tired, I take a rest at a truck stop. Then I am ready to go!

I keep you safe and sound.
While you are in bed, I patrol
the streets. I am ready to help
at all hours.

10

We are on the job all the time.
You may not need us, but we are
ready if you smell smoke!

I keep the presses going at a steady pace. A boy on a bicycle might bring the paper to your home. Your parents might read the front page at breakfast.

12

I work on television. If you
tune in, I'll tell you what is
happening. You'll find out how
to dress for the weather, too.

I work at a radio station. If you can't sleep, turn on your radio. I keep the tunes playing all night.

You need heat, lights, and
the telephone—even in the middle
of the night. We are here at
all hours.

You have read about some jobs. Your parents may do these jobs. You may want to have one of them when you grow up.